MY ALLAH SERIES
ALLAH GIVES US FOOD

KISA KIDS PUBLICATIONS

AL-KISA
FOUNDATION
WWW.KISAKIDS.ORG

PARENTS' CORNER

وَمَا مِن دَآبَّةٍ فِي الْأَرْضِ إِلَّا عَلَى اللّٰهِ رِزْقُهَا

There is no animal on the earth except that its sustenance lies with Allāh
(Sūrat Hūd, Verse 6)

Dear Parents/Guardians,

Allāh is our Rabb, Nurturer, and Provider. He created us and takes care of us. We see that He provides and takes care of every creature, even the smallest of them. It is very important to emphasize to your children that Allāh created us, loves us, and takes care of us. You see, when children realize that Allāh created them, their parents, all their favorite foods, and favorite animals, they will develop a sense of appreciation and gratitude towards Allāh. When children understand that Allāh is our Sustainer and takes care of us, this will help strengthen their love and need for Allāh. Together, these two qualities will allow children to make good choices that will please Allāh.

It is also important to help children realize that Allāh has created and allocated appropriate blessings for each creature to help it reach its full potential. The potential of the human being is to reach perfection and live its life in the servitude of Allāh. We should emphasize to our children that Allāh gives us all of these blessings so we are able to make good choices, become better people, get closer to Allāh, and attain His pleasure.

With Duʿas,
Kisa Kids Publications

Allah created many yummy foods for us to eat.
He created fruits, vegetables, nuts, and even meat!

What does your mom feed you?

Monkeys love sweet, yellow bananas, you see.
So, Allah filled the jungle with delicious banana trees.

What are some other things monkeys need?
Who provides it for them?

Ants love to eat yummy seeds and tiny grains. So, Allah gave them plenty — a little to eat now and some for when it rains!

Look at the little ant. How is he carrying the seed?

Whales in the ocean need lots of fish and krill to eat. So, Allah filled the waters with these delicious treats.

How many fish do you think a whale needs to eat?

6

Giraffes love to eat large green leaves.
So, Allah gave them long necks to reach for the trees.

How do the long necks help the giraffes?
Who gave them the special long necks?

Camels in dry deserts love to eat grass.
So, Allah put it in places that they are sure to pass.

What do you think would happen to the camels if Allah didn't make grass in the desert?

Birds fly around, looking for worms to grab and pick.
So, Allah gave them wings to help them find food for their chicks.

Why are the baby chicks opening their mouths?

Hungry lions hunt to get meat they love to eat.
So, Allah gave them claws, paws, and super sharp teeth!

*What did Allah give the donkey to be able to run away
quickly from the hungry lion?*

Rabbits love to eat carrots that are orange, long, and big.
So, Allah created carrots in the ground for them to claw and dig.

How many rabbits and carrots do you see in the picture?

Allah even takes care of the little babies, you know!
He gives their mommies milk, so they can become strong and grow.

Allah remembers everyone, and gives them what they need.
He does not need anything, it is us that He feeds!

What are some things Allah has given you?